Zentangle Fantasy

AN INTRICATE ADULT COLORING BOOK

A fantastical collection of beautifully drawn creatures to stimulate your creativity, increase your focus and improve your fine motor skills.

Fine tip markers are ideal for these designs.

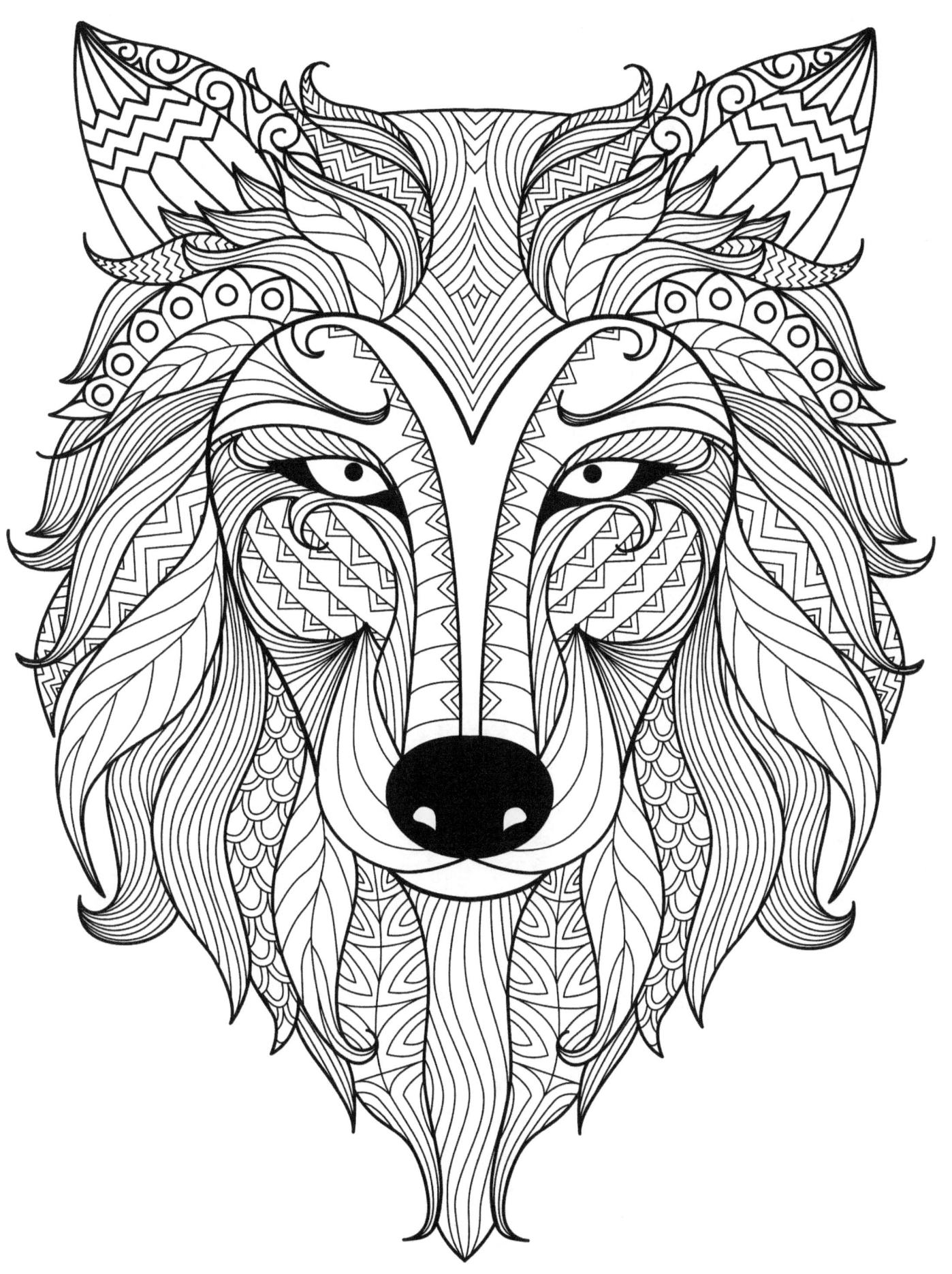

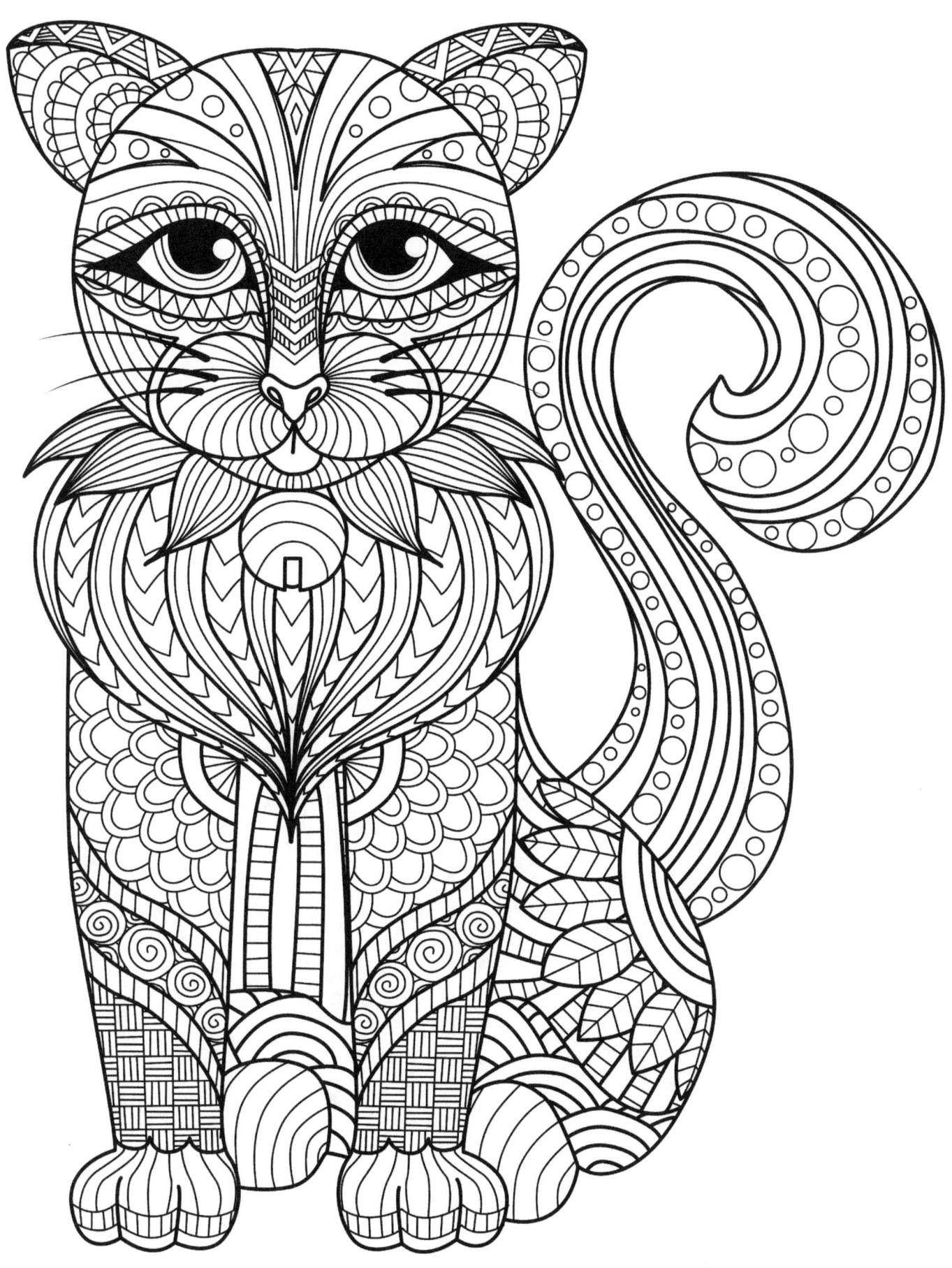

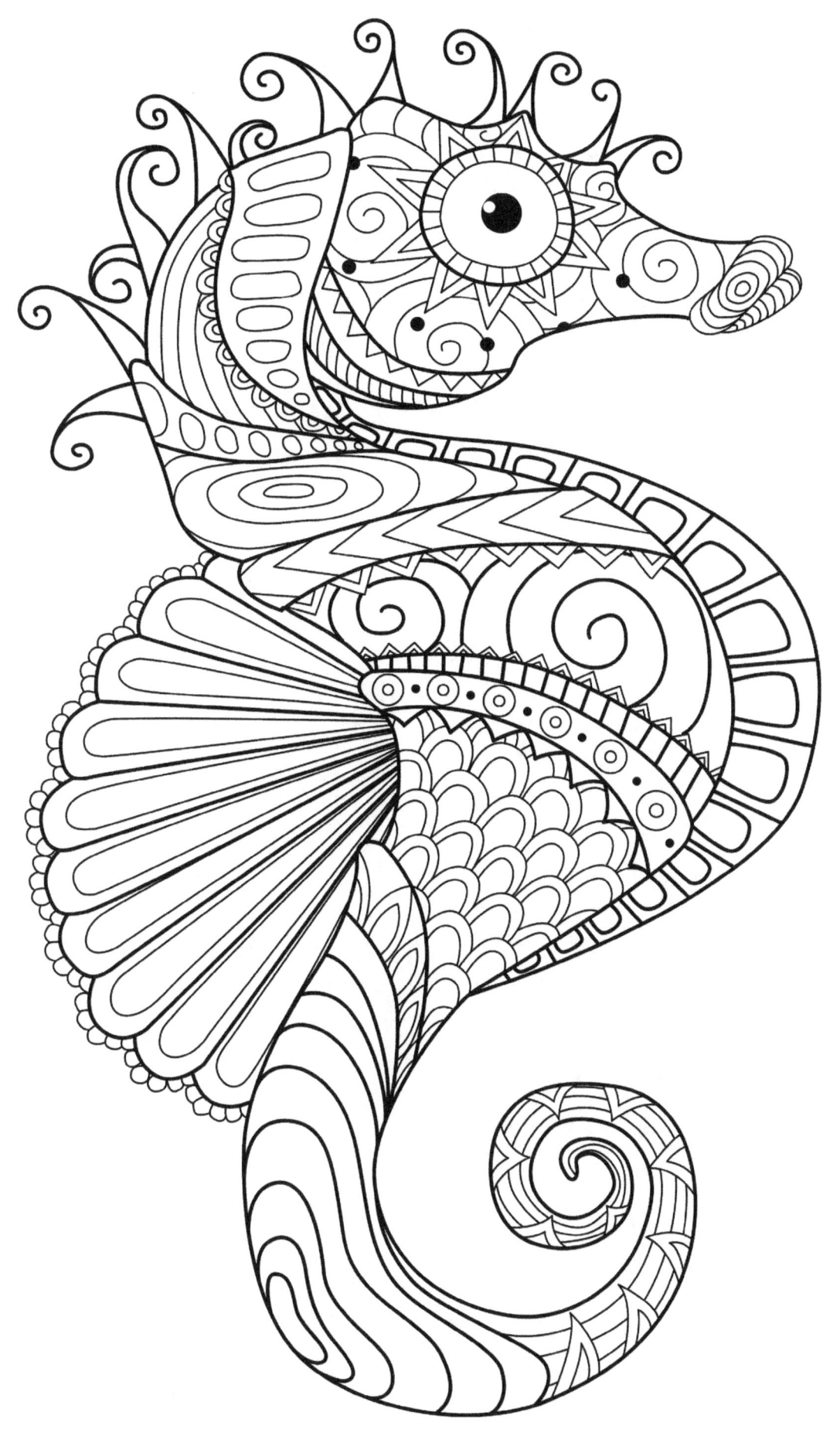

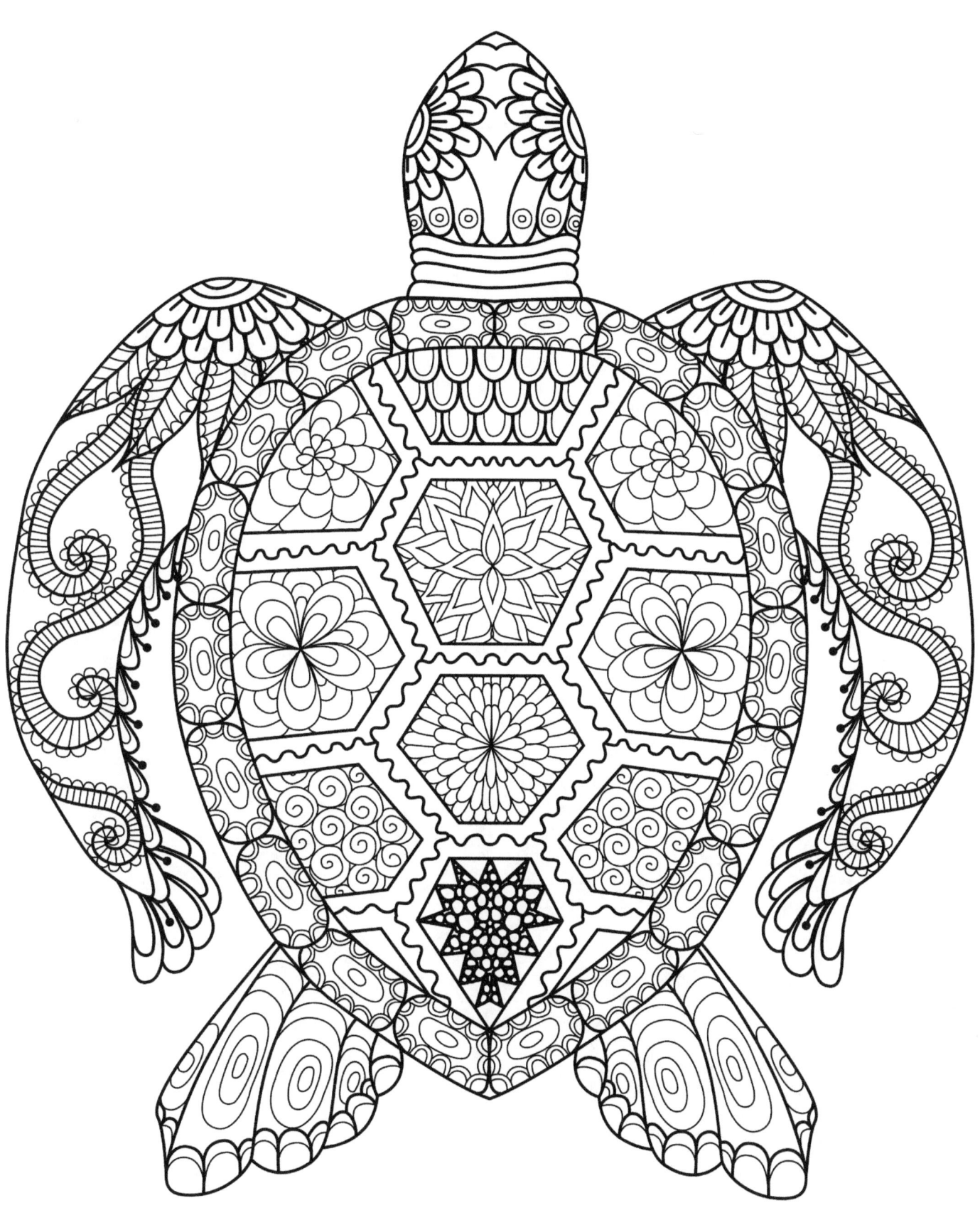

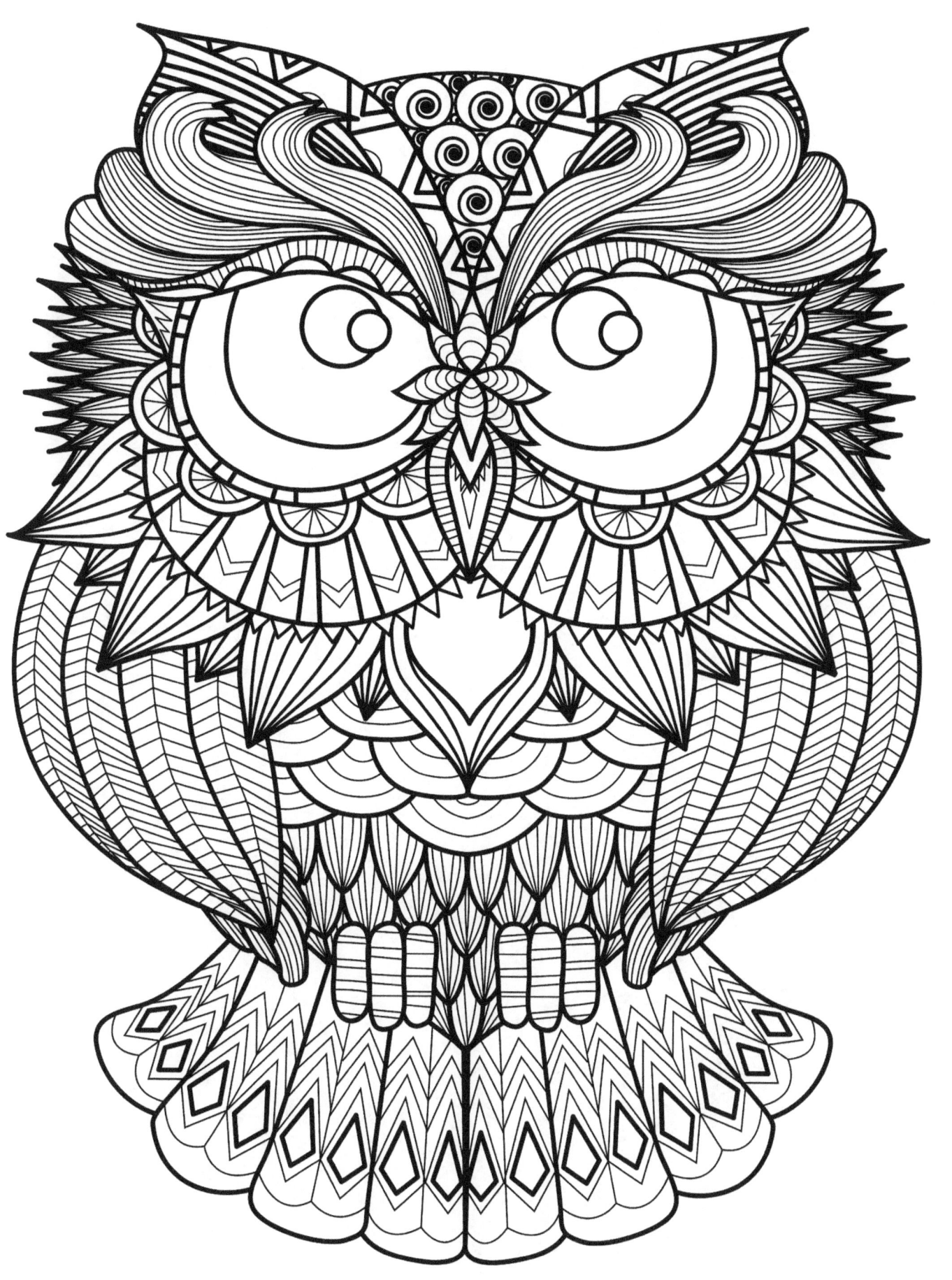

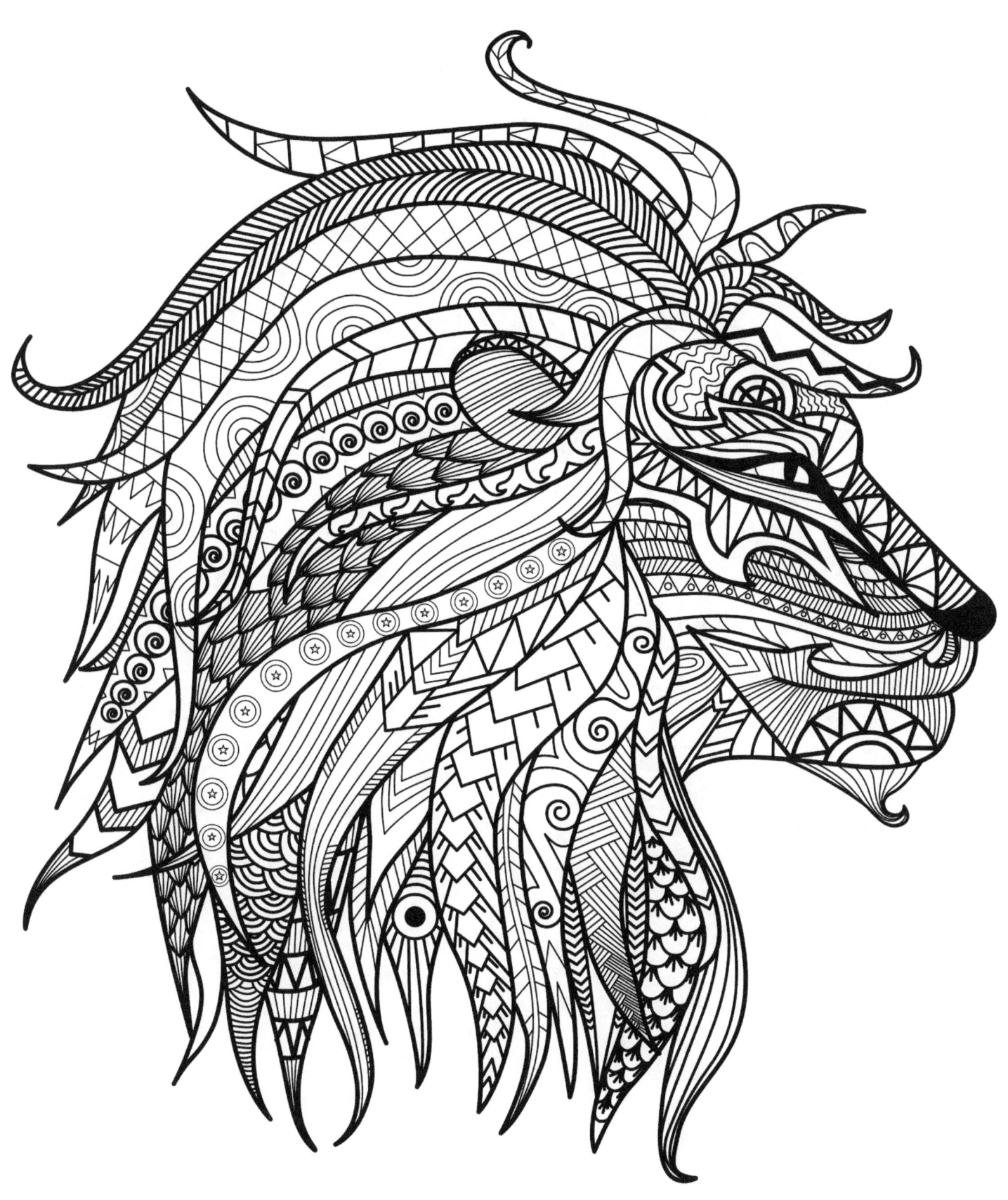

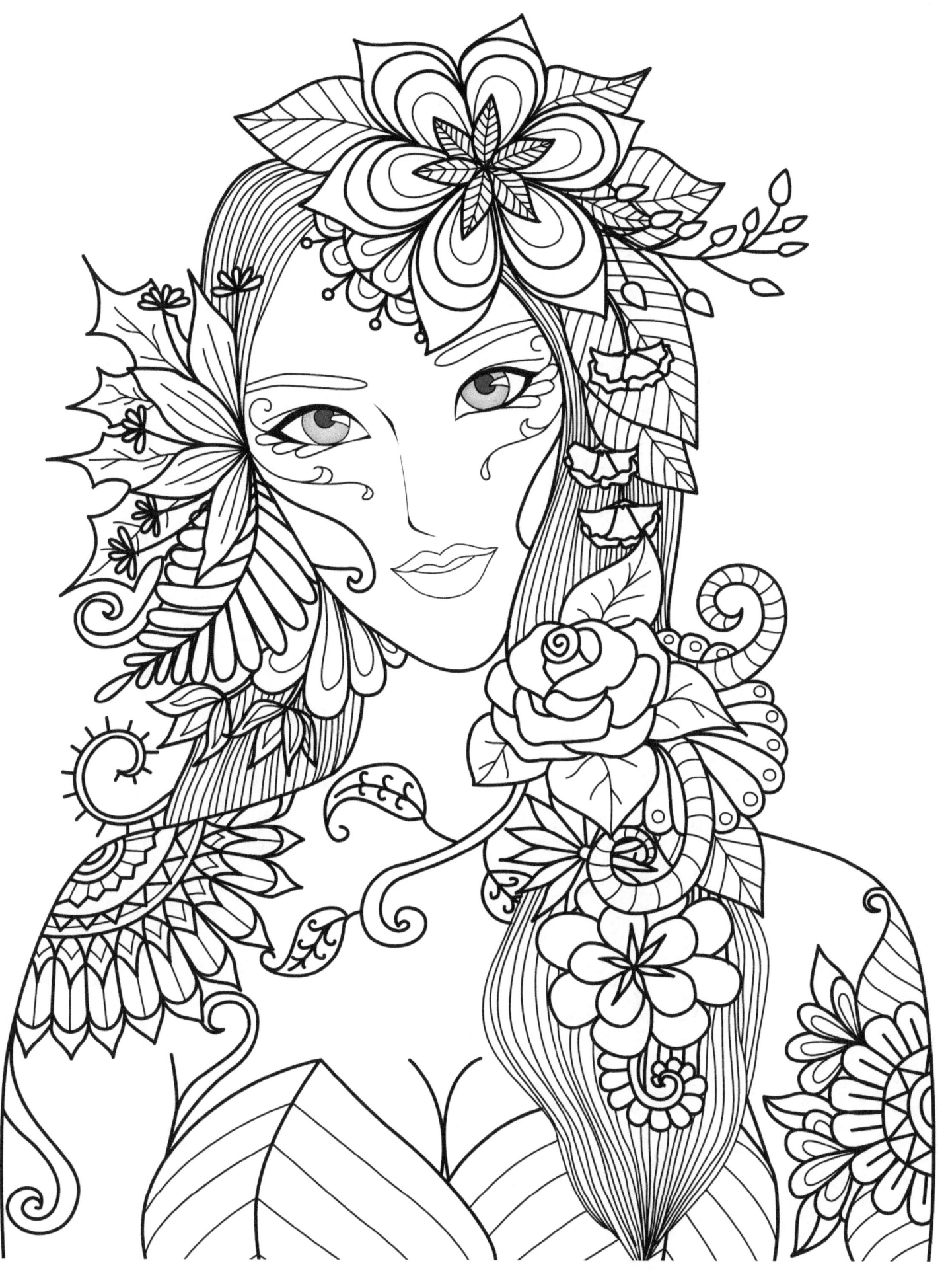

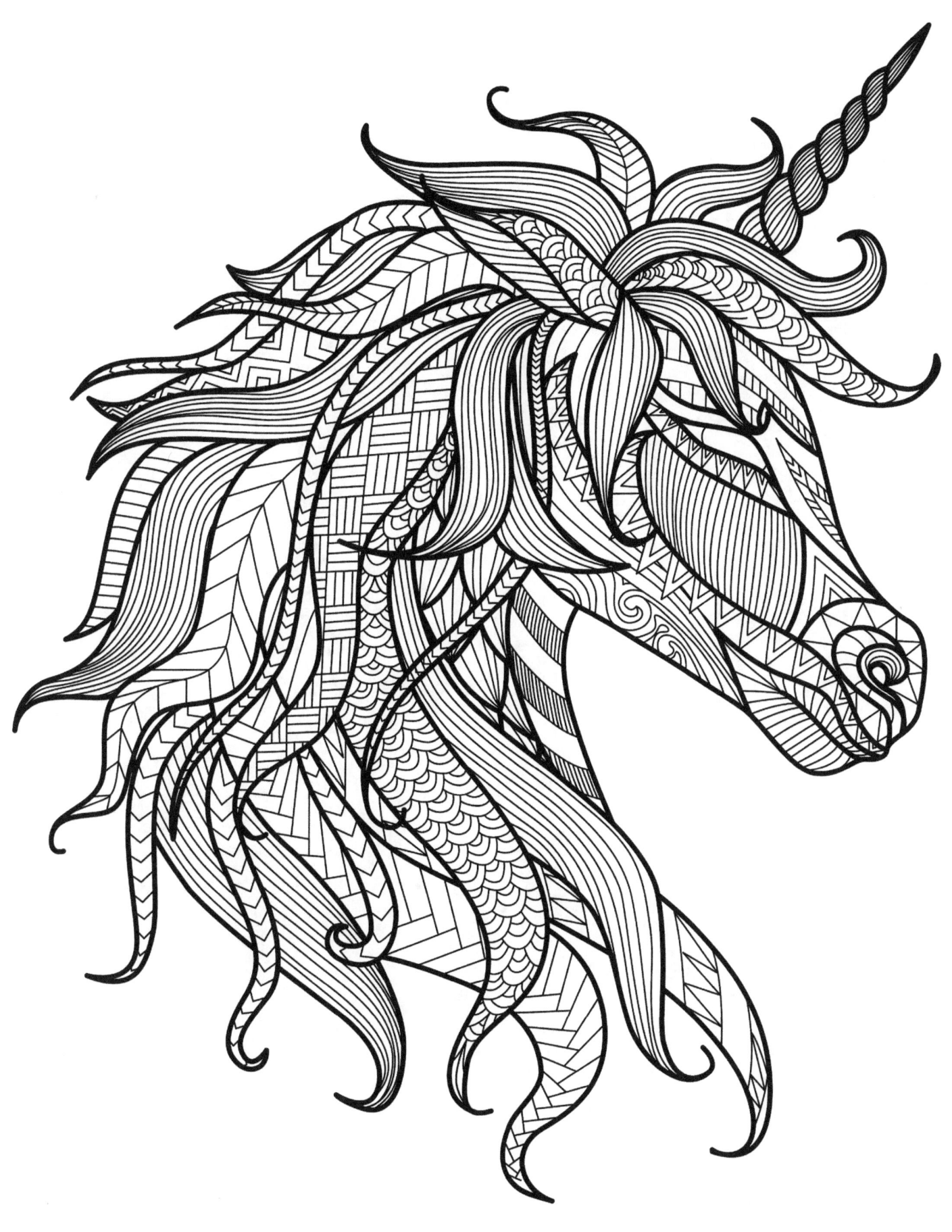

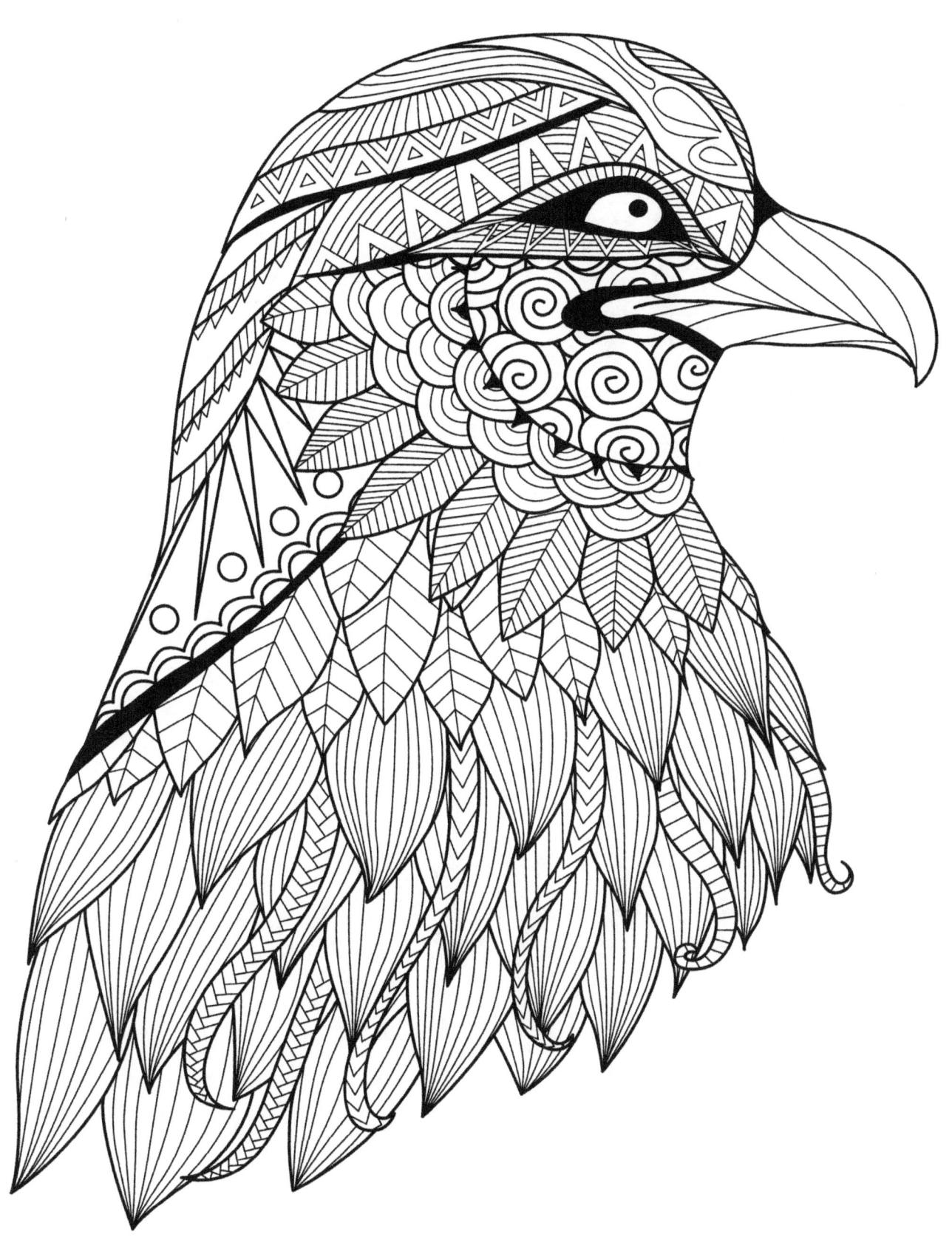

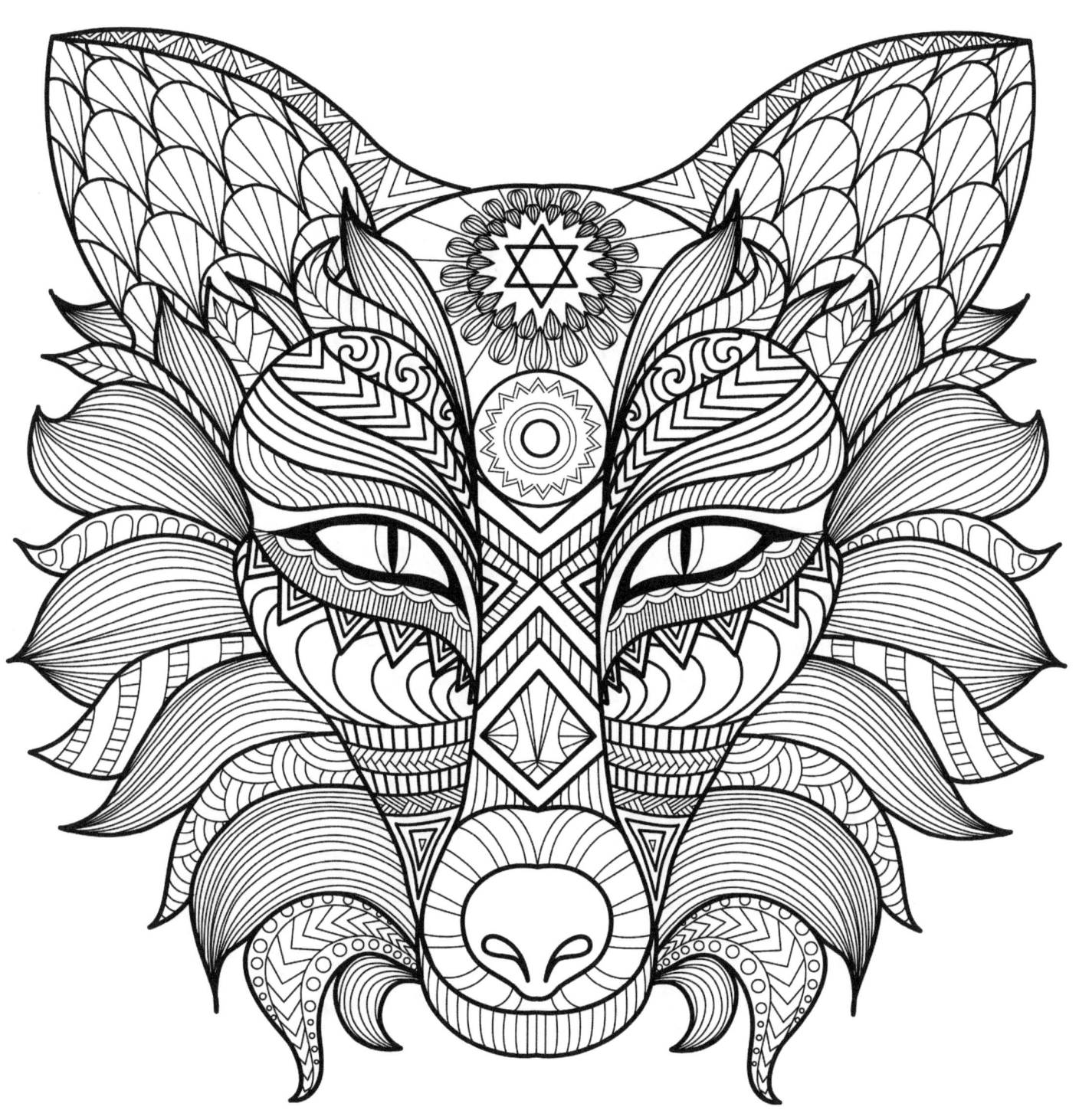

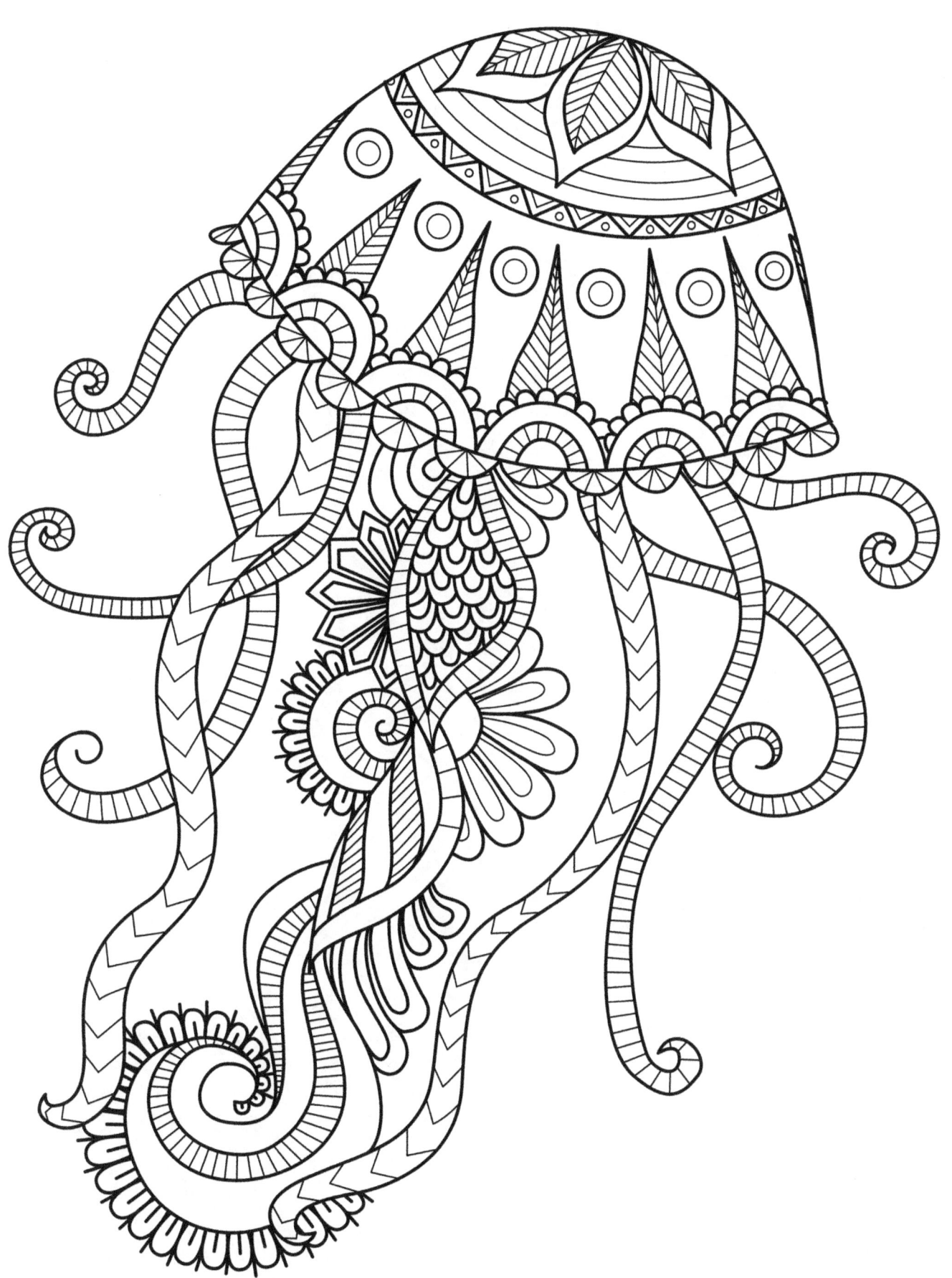

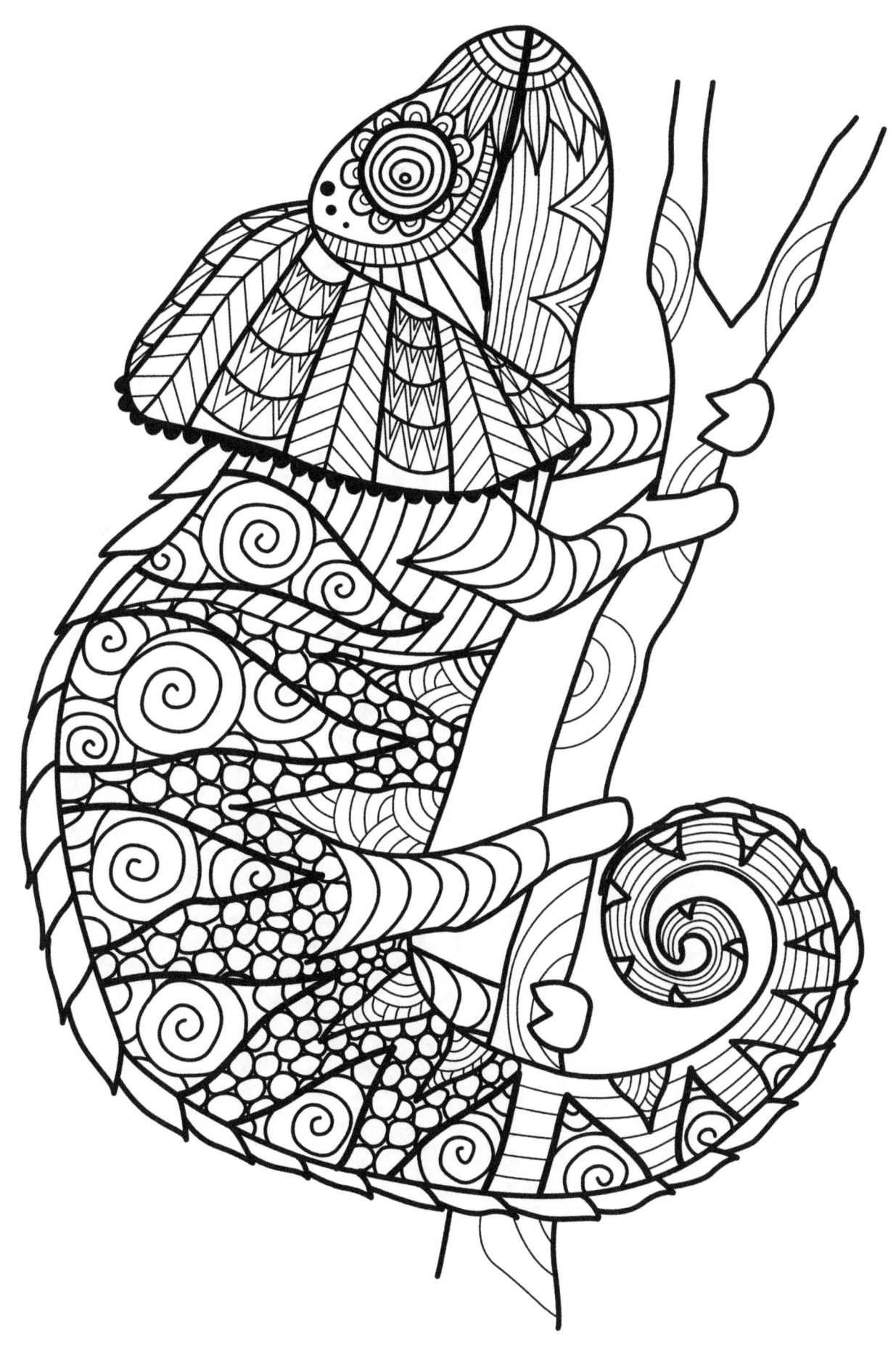

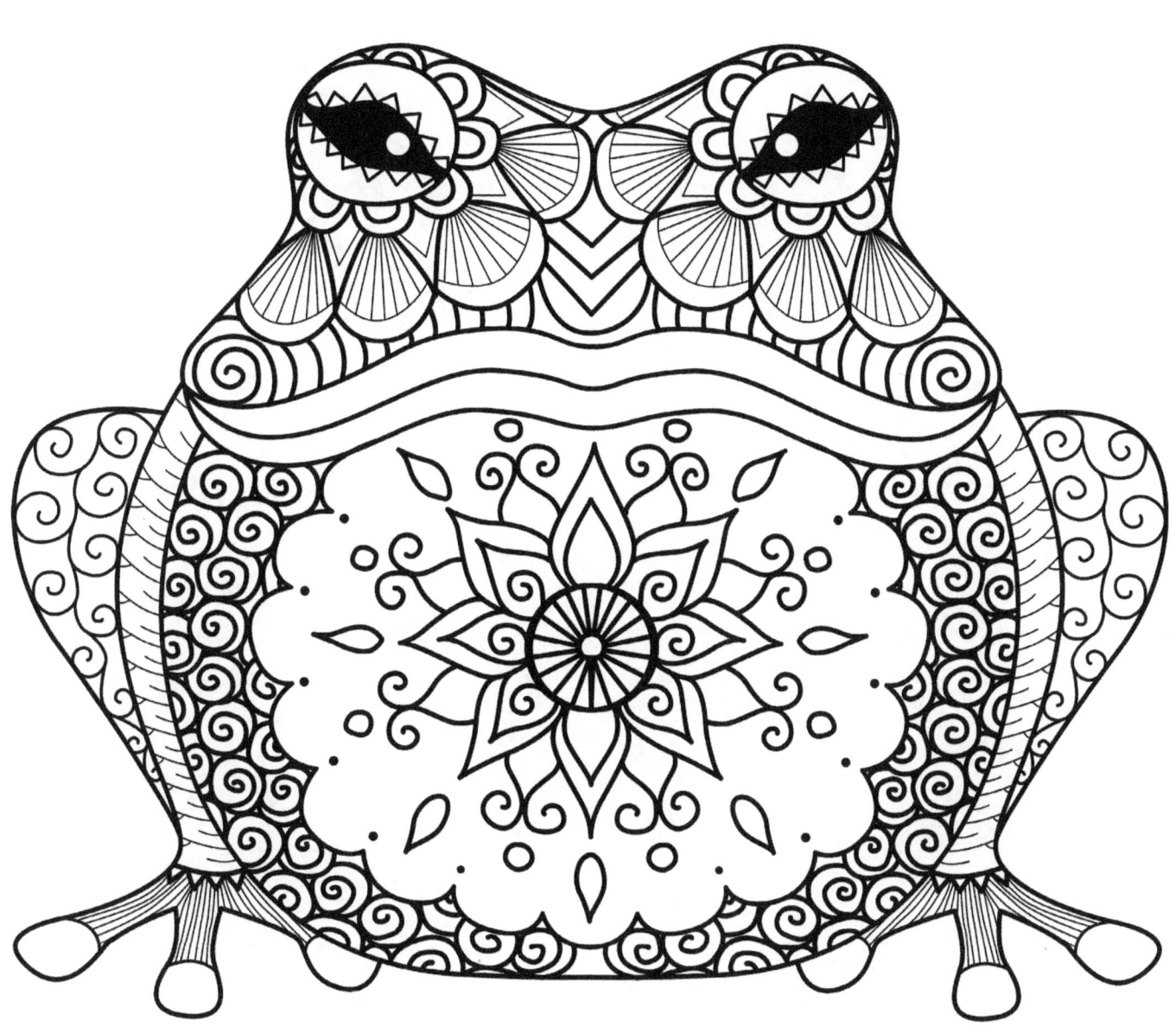

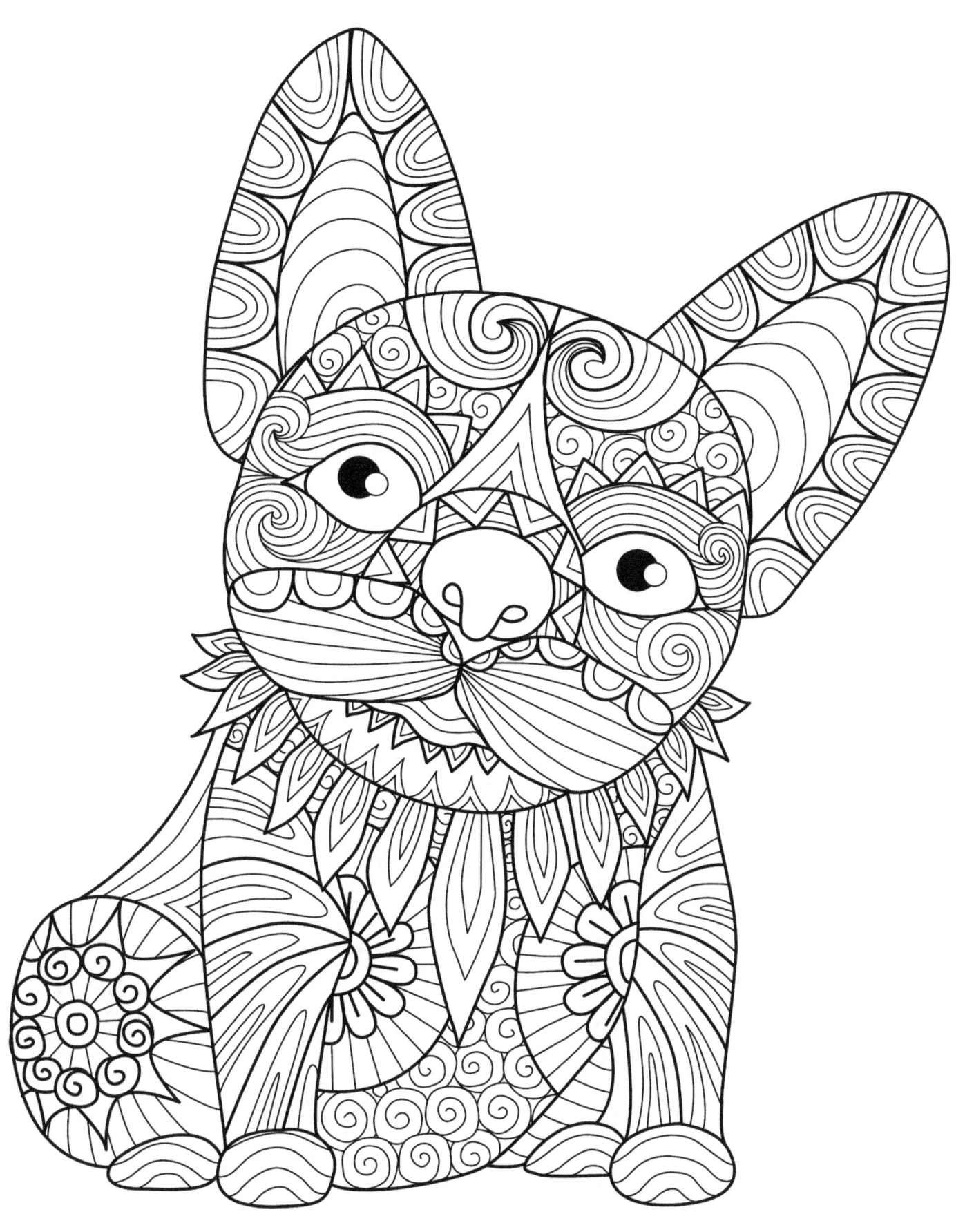

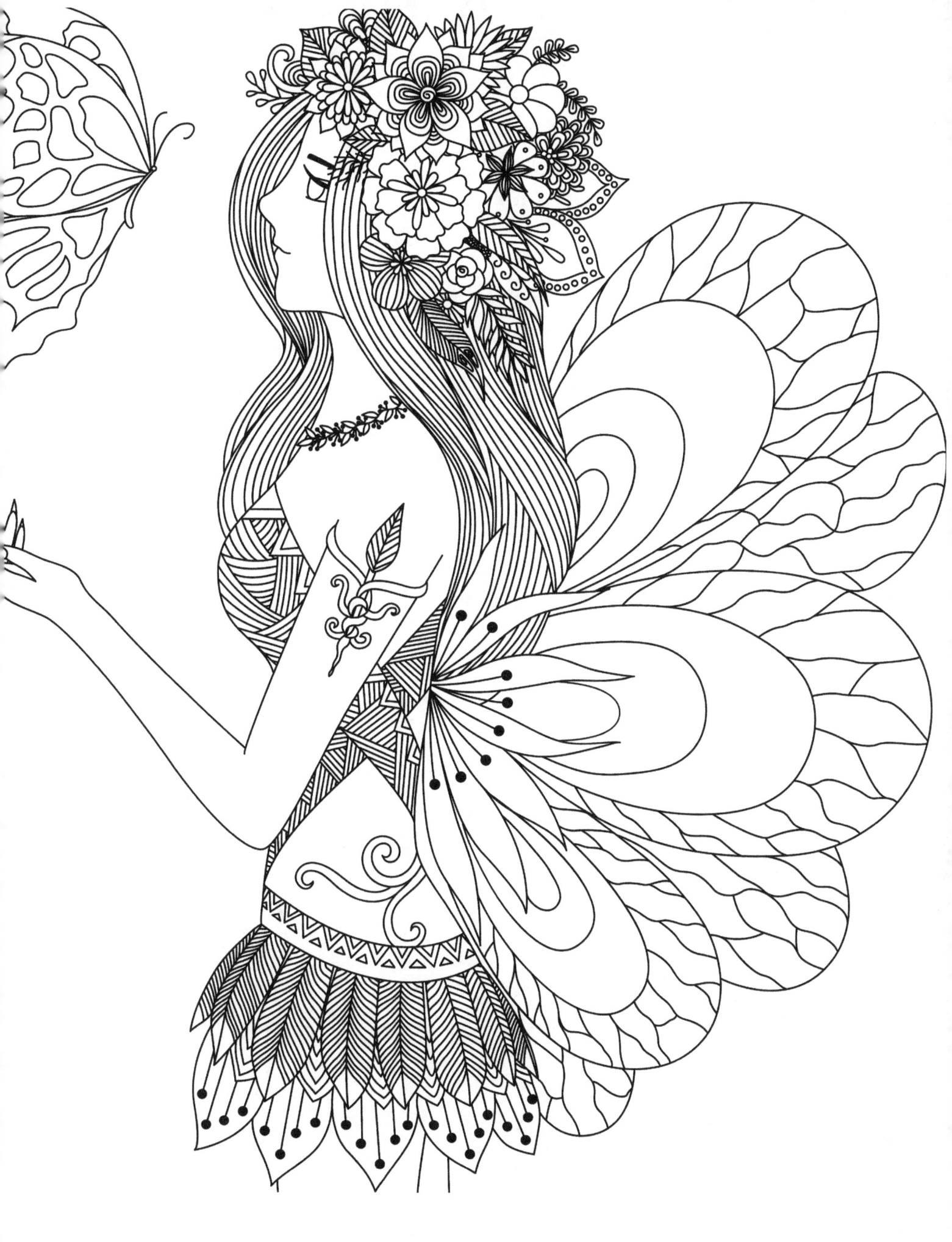

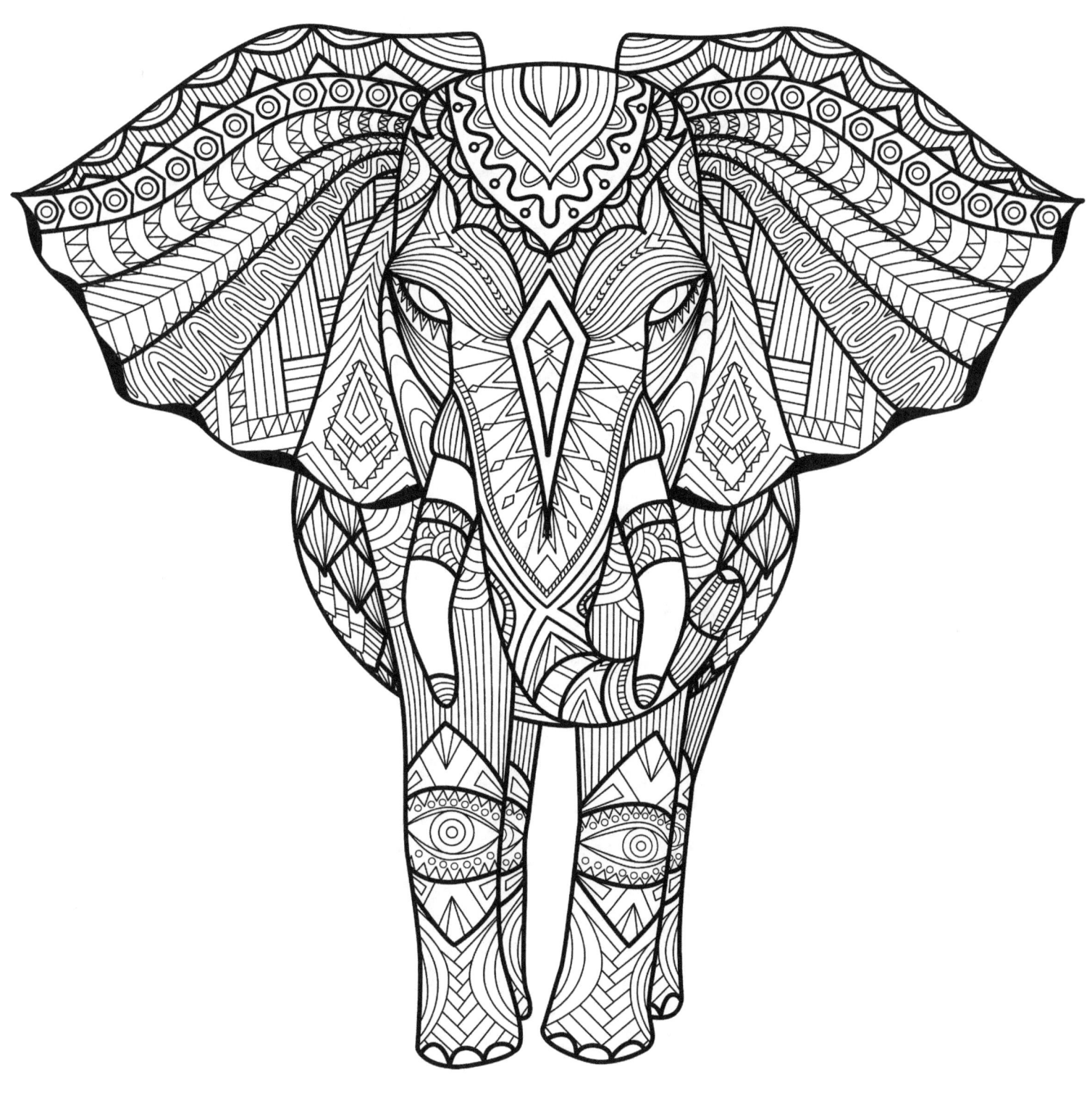

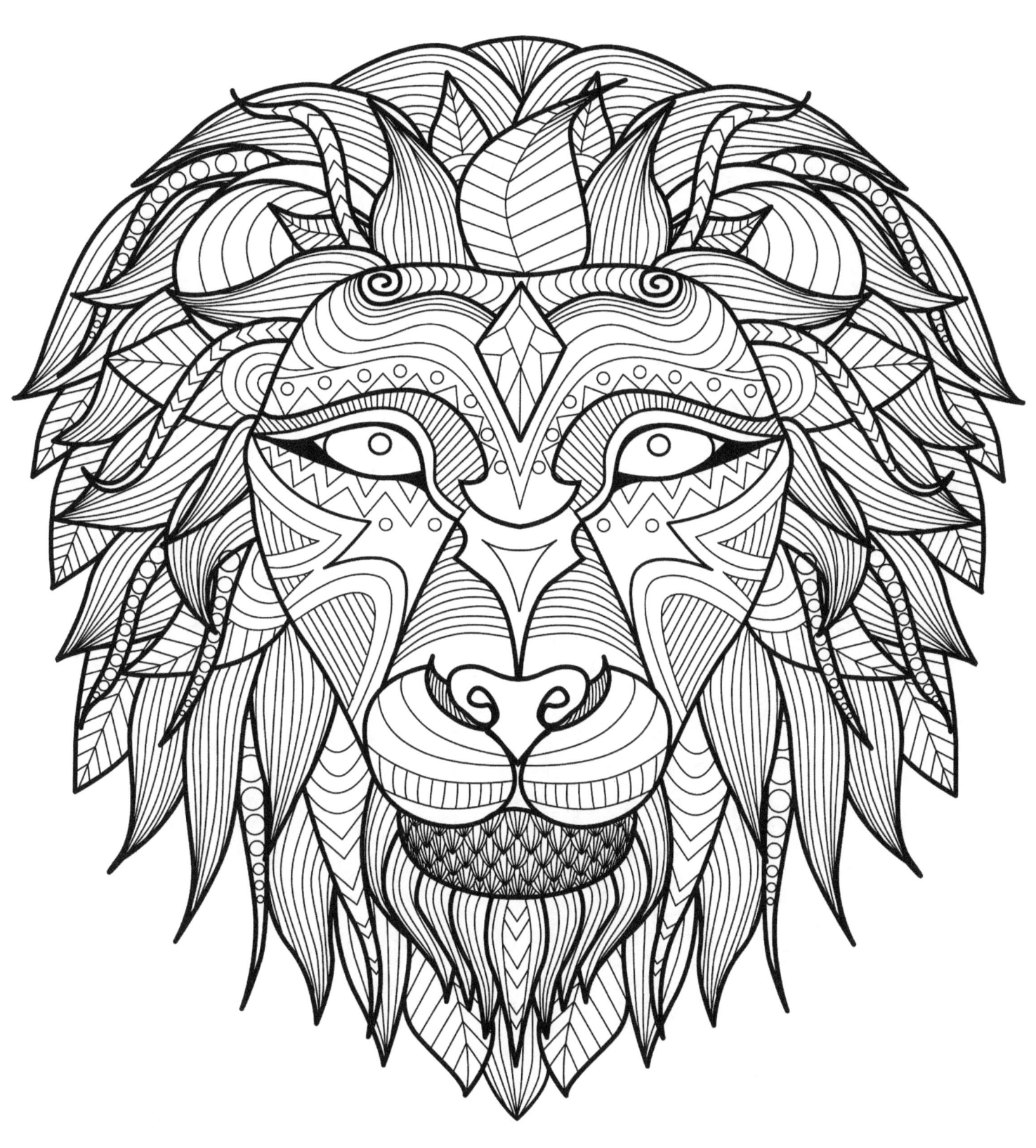

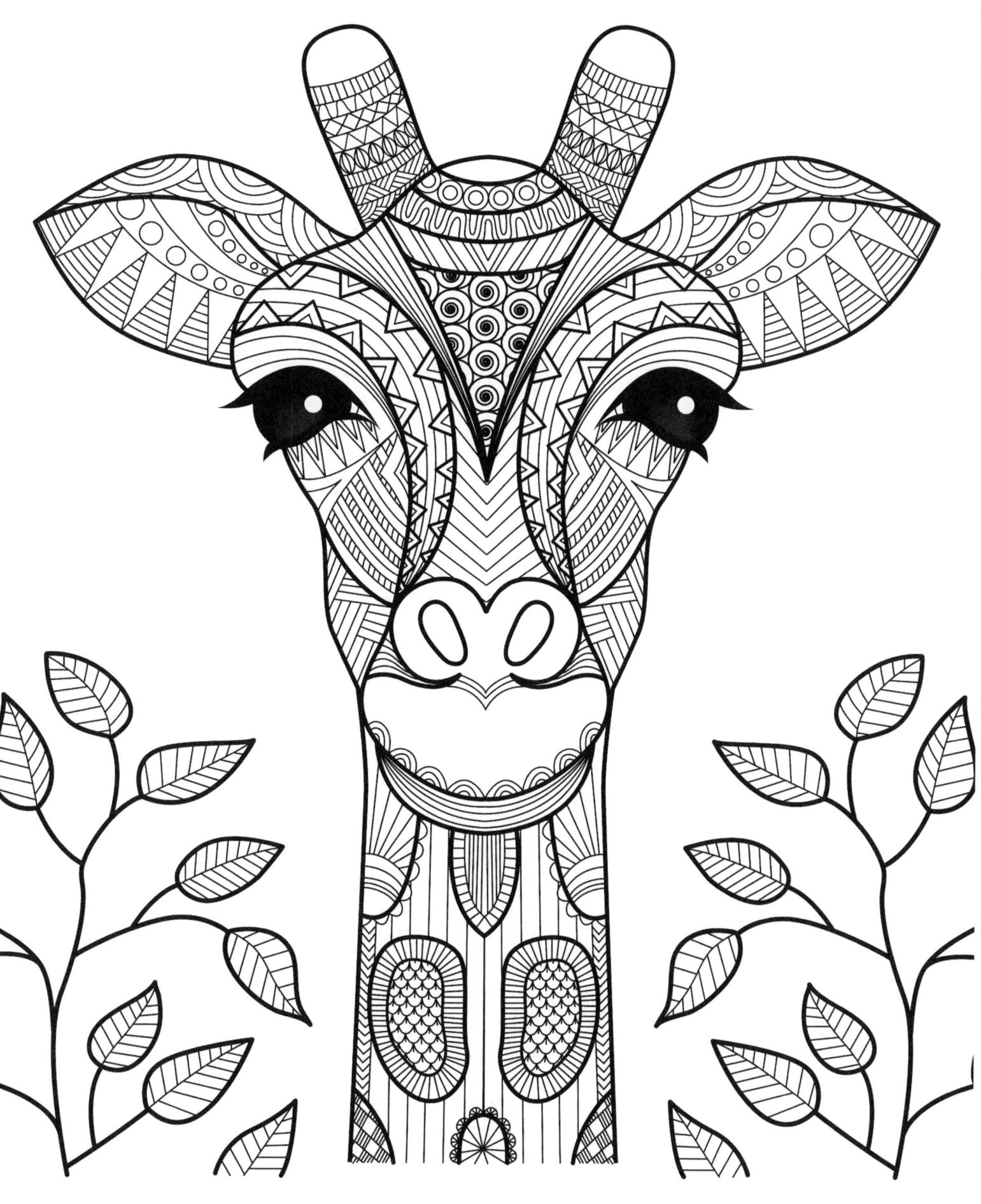

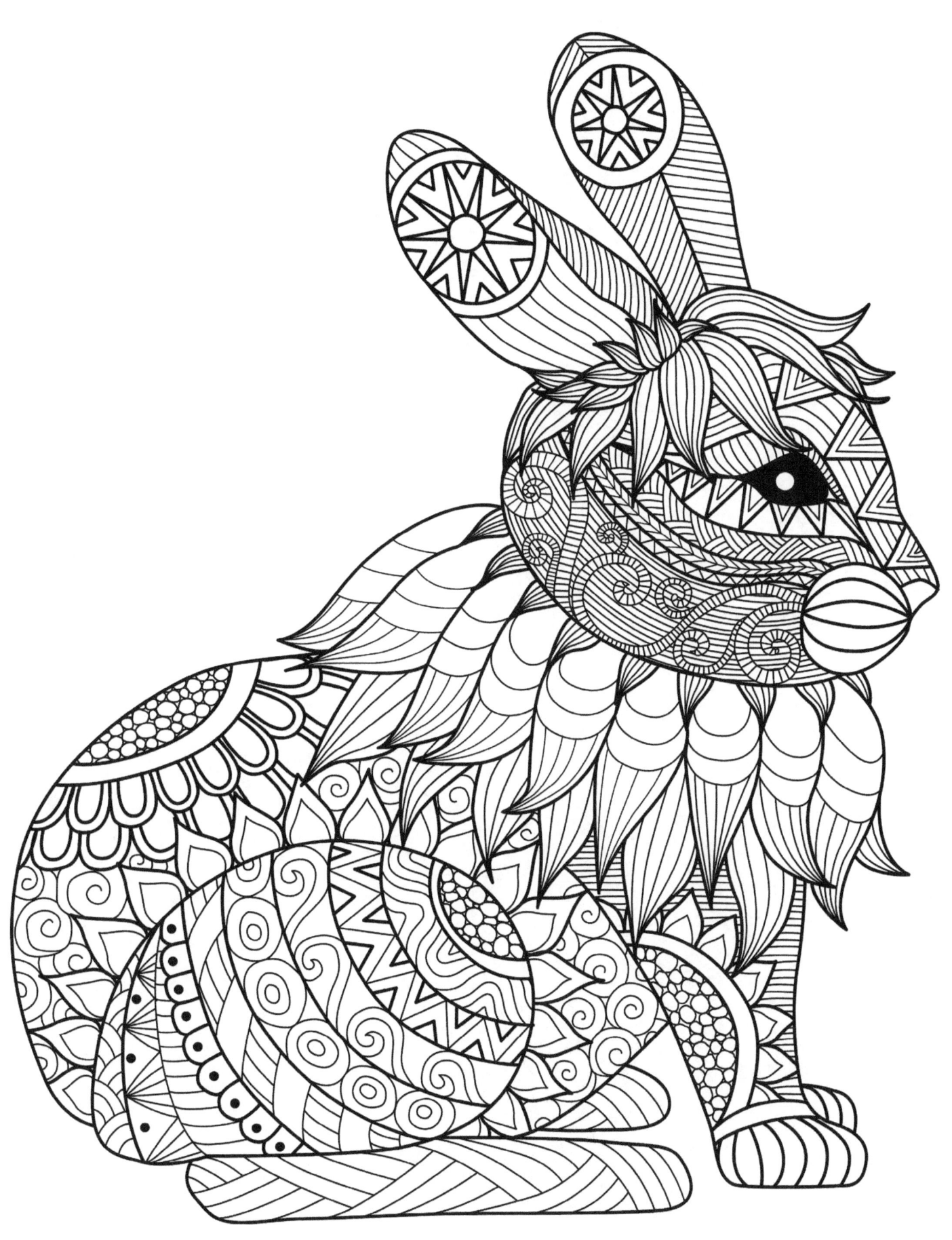

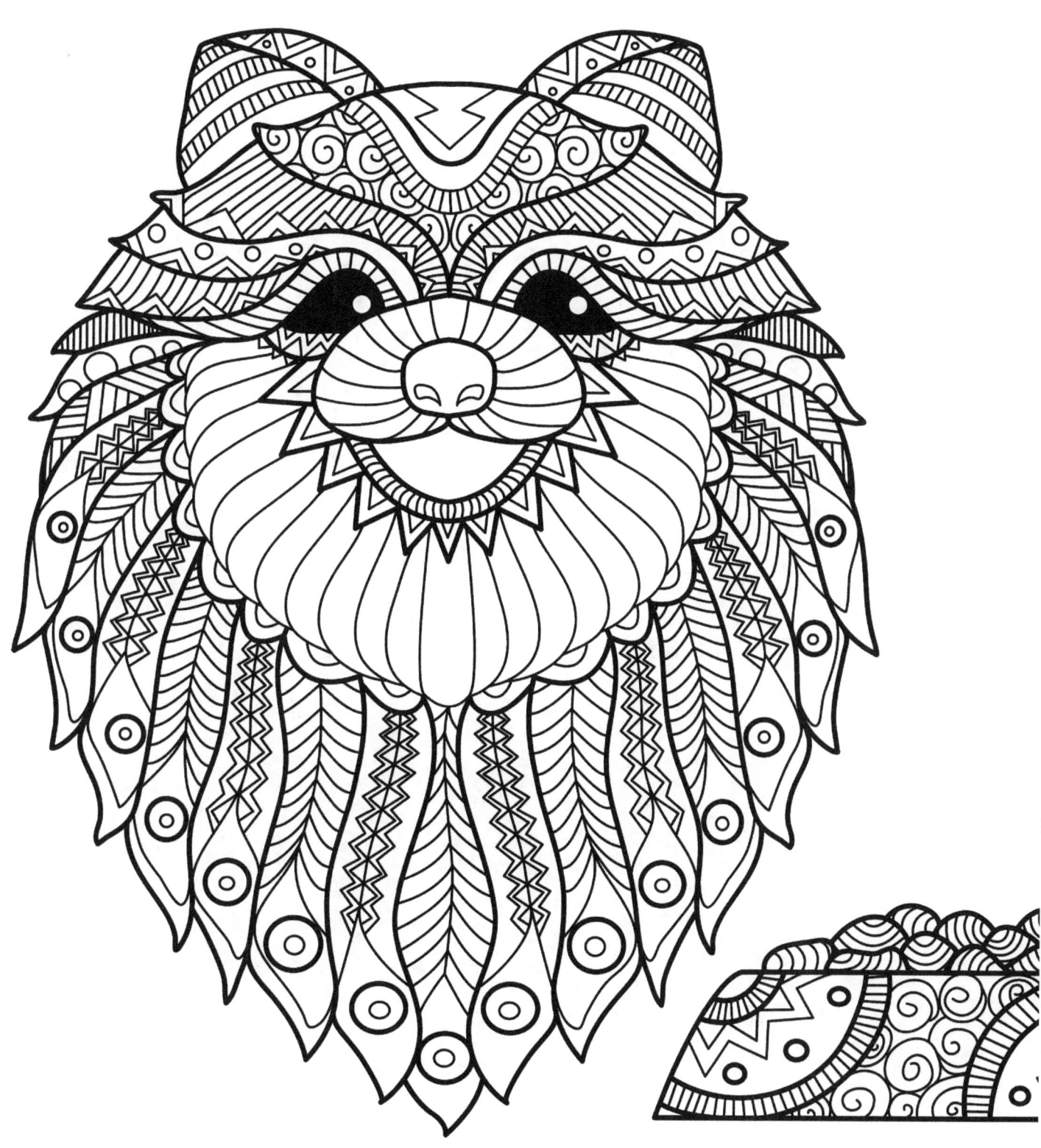

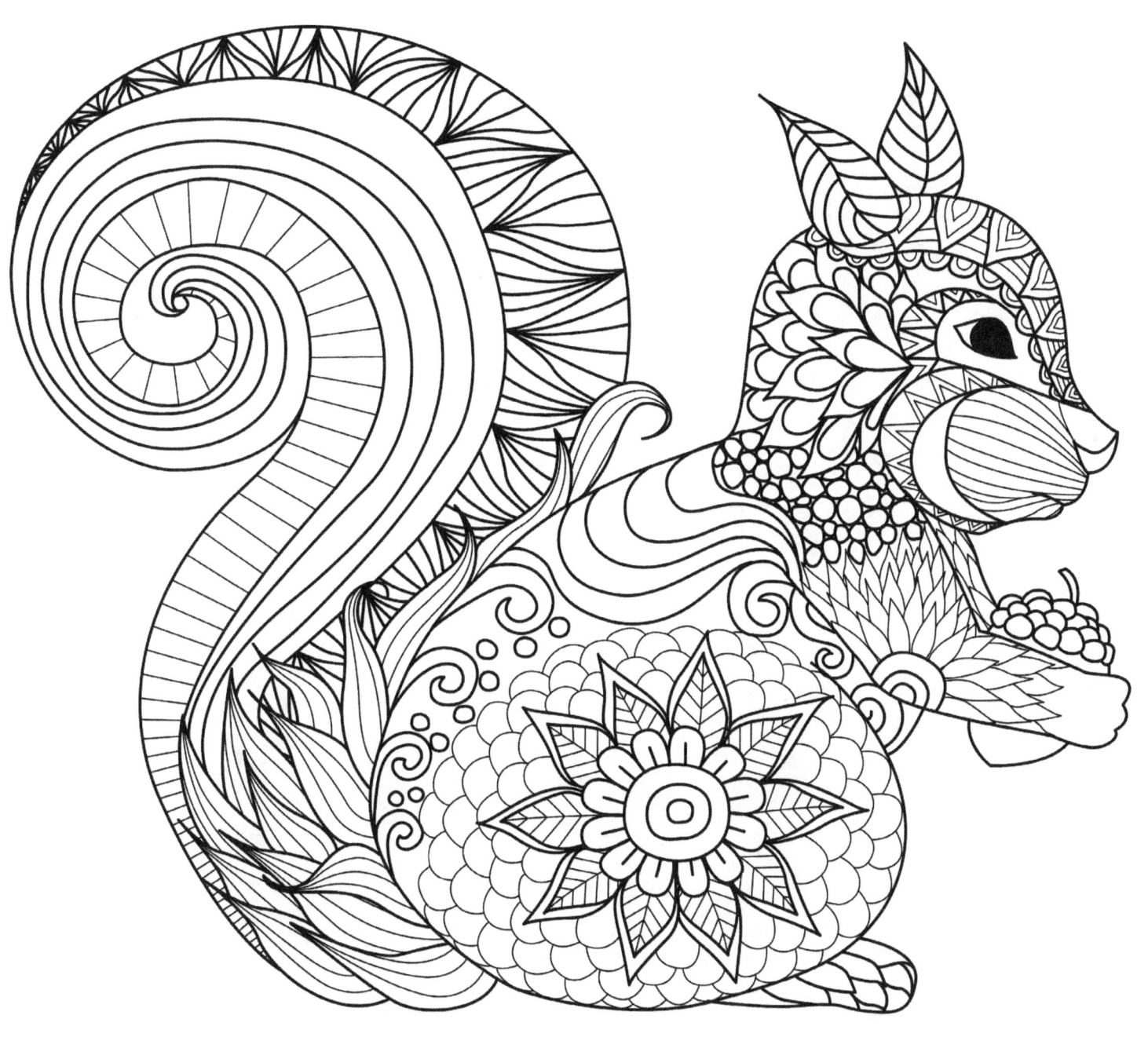

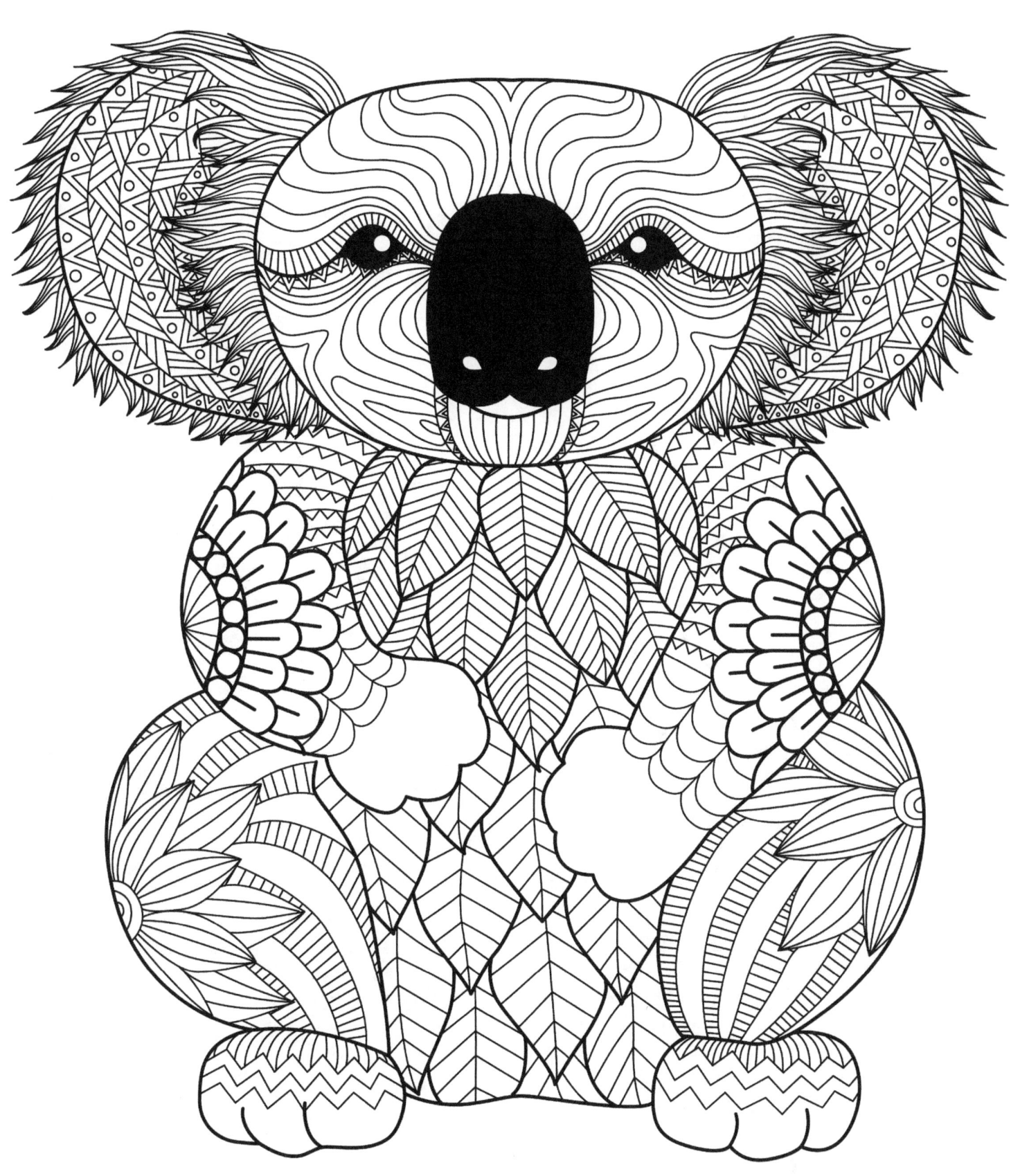